Little Wonders: A reflection on early motherhood

Hannah Richards

BookLeaf Publishing

Presentation by *BookLeaf Publishing*

Web: www.bookleafpub.com

E-mail: info@bookleafpub.com

ISBN: 978-93-95755-47-4

First edition 2022

For Rowan - I love you.

ACKNOWLEDGEMENT

There are several people I need to thank, for both their encouragement with these poems and their support for me in general.

First, my husband, Josh - a wonderful father and an incredible source of strength and reason when I'm struggling.
Secondly, my sister, Rachel - I could not ask for a more enthusiastic and selfless supporter.
Thirdly, my parents, Lynda and Brett - they have been there whenever I've needed help, a hug, a babysitter, or anything else I could possibly need.

There are so many people who have been there to offer support through my parenting journey and through my pregnancy loss. My wonderful in-laws, my beautiful friends, and my terrific mother's group - all have made me laugh, smile and give thanks for the people in my life.

PREFACE

When I first began writing these poems, I was almost through my first year of parenthood. I had experienced a love beyond imagining with my baby boy, but was also deep in the midst of post-natal anxiety. Writing about my feelings and experiences from the beginning of my pregnancy and through the first year of my son's life allowed me to reflect on the beauty and challenges I was facing. Poetry is the perfect medium for exploring emotions and processing experiences.

Later, I lost my second pregnancy, which would have been another little boy. Around this time, the opportunity to write more of these poems arose and I took the chance to process the new grief and loss that I was feeling through words.

These poems are written in two separate parts. The first 18 poems are about pregnancy, birth and the first year with my little boy. They are about him and for him. The final three poems are written about my second pregnancy, that I lost at 14 weeks. These final poems are not for everyone, and some readers may prefer to stop after "Dear Baby". There is no right or wrong way to deal with a loss, and it's up to each individual to decide what will or will not help them.

Parenthood is such a roller coaster of pain, joy, stress, excitement and every emotion imaginable. I hope that any parent reading these poems will find some sense of connection to the words and feel less alone. Everyone's experiences are their own, but it helps to know that others go through similar challenges. I also hope that anyone struggling is able to read here how every day is worth it for the beautiful gift of loving a child.

Positive?

Positive? It's positive!
Wait, are we sure?
Test again, test again…
Positive!

Let's tell the world
No, wait - too soon
Let's just the two of us share this moment
Or three of us now?

Joy, panic, this feels kind of weird
Does everyone go through this?
Every movement must be careful!
Every moment feels unreal

Positive?
Doc says it's positive!
Okay, now it's really real
Happiness, stress, excitement, fear

Yes, Mum, it's true
I know, I can't believe it either
Your tears are my tears
Only eight more months to wait

Only eight months!

So much still to do!
Names? Clothes? A nursery?
Wait - just breathe

A poppyseed
That's how small you are
You've turned our world over
Eight more months of this roller coaster

But you'll be perfect
I'm positive

Pop

Collapsing on my mattress
Weary from another day
Contemplating so many more months

Pop
Is that you?

Not this soon, I tell myself
And a few more weeks go by
Waiting for the first twelve weeks to end

Pop, flutter
Is that you?

Maybe, but how to know?
I've never done this before
A few more days and weeks pass by

Flutter, flutter
I think that's you!

Weary wonder
Nauseous excitement
One hand resting gently

Nudge
Hi there, you!

I never knew before right now
How much love could be felt
In a tiny, little nudge

The wonder grows
As you do, too
Moving and stretching inside

Keep growing little bump!

Kick
Ouch!

Unsolicited

"You're so big!"
"You're so small!"
"Soon you'll hardly sleep at all!"
"Are you ready?"
"All prepared?"
"If I were you, I'd be so scared!"

Touch my belly
Feel him kick
Can't say no, they're just too quick
Can't be angry
"It's not real
Hormones change the way you feel"

"Can you eat that?"
"Put that down!"
"You'll get hurt carrying things around!"
"You'll have stretch marks"
"And saggy tits!"
"Have fun finding clothes that fit!"

Body's changing
Said goodbye
Okay with it, but that's a lie
But it's awesome

What it can do
One day I'll love the new me too

Advice and comments
From strangers and friends
Flooding in until pregnancy ends
Won't be over
When the baby's here
No, this is just the start, I fear

Welcome

Hidden behind a blue curtain
Strange sounds and conversation
A hush
Everyone's waiting
Then we hear a sudden cry

The most awaited sound, for certain
And once it starts it doesn't stop
So beautiful
Then we see you
Over the curtain, held up high

Welcome, little one, nice to meet you
And wow! Such big feet!
Turning pink
Still screaming
As you're cleaned and wrapped up tight

Placed on my chest so we can greet you
Is that a dimple on your chin?
So small
A magical moment
Now everything seems right

Recovery while you're weighed

Much bigger than we'd thought!
First breastfeed
The first of so many
Connection forming with my son

Family arrives in an awed parade
We couldn't be more thrilled
Our baby
We've all been waiting
Welcome to the world, little one

Snuggle Close

It's okay, beautiful
Mummy's here
To calm your cries
And hold you near

Just close your eyes
And snuggle close
Know you're the one
I love the most

One little hand
Lay on my chest
Your gentle suckling
At my breast

I brush your hair
And gaze on down
As you relax
That tiny frown

Your eyes drift shut
Your breathing slows
Tears all gone
As are your woes

Sleeping now
All cuddled in
Stay right here
My sweet munchkin

I'll hold you tight
Sleep here on me
For far too soon
Grown up you'll be

Now for tonight
There's no more tears
Sleep soundly, love
Your Mummy's here

Rainbow Days

Some days are like rainbows
Pure, glistening, bright
The colours wash through everything
My heart is full of light

Red is how he makes a mess
With strawberries and tomato
Little hands waving about
Rosy cheeks a-glow

Orange is the sunrise
He slumbers next to me
The sun rays lighten up the room
As he dreams peacefully

Yellow is his perfect smile
And soft hair, spun like gold
Cheeky giggles fill the house
Such wonder to behold

Green is walking around together
Grassy parks and trees
Seeing the world through brand new eyes
Flowers swaying in the breeze

Blue is the colour of his eyes
Exactly the same as mine
Watching, learning, following along
They sparkle and shine

Indigo is our goodnight
The quiet and the moon
Precious kisses and stories
Snug like a cocoon

Violet is singing songs with him
We've one for everything
Bath time, play time, just for fun
He loves it when we sing

Some days are like rainbows
They stand out from the rest
The days when it's all worth it
And I feel so very blessed

A Quiet Night

Resting darkness surrounds
A husband's quiet snores
A gentle background rhythm
As a mother gazes through the night
Her eyes adjusted to the gloom
For awake she has sat
An hour or more

Sweet infant curled at her breast
His breathing fast
Beside his father's slow pace
He suckles a while, frantic
Then pauses in the quiet
Then returns to his feed
Eyes closed, content and safe

The mother waits patiently
Stroking her child's soft hair
Her calm gaze tracing lines
Of moonlit shadows against the walls
She sits and waits
Alone here in her alertness
But she feels not alone

For as she follows the moonlight

She wonders to herself
How many others
Are sitting in this moment
Awake in the darkness
Holding children close
As they drift into deeper sleep?

There are mothers all over
In the deep of the night
Connected through the darkness
Watching silver glimmers of light
Stroking precious cheeks
Listening to those snores
And waiting for the sunrise

Deprivation

Dragging chains weigh on me
Each moment draws my last reserves
Down
I'm falling down again
No fight left
No more strength

A cry so small pierces my heart
Pushes against the heaviness
Blink
I'm blinking in the dark
Lift the chains
Carry them

A cargo more valuable than life
But the ship is trying to sink
Dark
Moments of dark descend
Push away
Bring back the light

Dragging chains around again
Struggling against their weight
Love
My love needs me here

There's still strength left
To win tonight

Peaceful darkness here at last
My love against my breast
Sleep
Sleep here with me tonight
Let strength return
Through pleasant dreams

Good Morning

The sun wakes up and so do you
Another day begins
With morning snuggles, a nappy change
And your beautiful, cheeky grin

Breakfast for the both of us
You sit in your high chair
Throwing food all over the floor,
And getting it in your hair

I'd love to have a nice, hot shower
Enjoying time solo
But no, you've found me once again
So I shut off the water flow

How about we sing some songs?
Your little hands start clapping
How many verses will you want
Until it's time for napping?

That spider climbs his water spout
Ducklings return to Mother
Five speckled frogs jump in the pool
"Galumph!" says another

It's time to rest your sleepy head
Your eyes close and I kiss you
Alone, I wait for you to wake
For when you sleep, I miss you

Dark Days

Some days are dark days
Thunder and blackened skies
It's hard, so hard
To feel the dark
Shadows
Inside

He smiles but the heavy weight
Smothers that little spark
It's dark, too dark
To smile back
To sing
And laugh

He cries and I cry with him
Fuelling the whirling torrent
Scream, we scream
Together
My heart
Hurts

He fights against me
At feeds, changes and baths
Breathe, breathe deep
Frustration builds

I fight
For calm

His dad comes home from work
I lash out with harsh words
Unfair, it's not fair
I'm not angry
With him
Just myself

Strength

He picks up the pieces
When he walks in the door
Puts me back together
Where I lay on the floor
A bright point of reason
When everything seems lost
He's the one person
Who loves me the most

At times it's so easy
To be caught in the whirlwind
Of day-to-day life
Feeling trapped and pinned
He's the one who breaks free
Of the pattern's repeat
Makes plans and moves forward
Turns bitter days sweet

He shoulders the weight
At the end of each day
And always forgives
The harsh words that I say
Not the cause of my ire
But the place where it lands
He returns it with love

Because he understands

He saves me so often
It doesn't seem fair
Through the dark and the bright days
He'll forever be there
Only one vow he made me
And this it stays true
To love me always
From the day we said "I do"

Guilty

The curse of a mother
Each day and each night
Despite all of the hard work
I feel bound up tight
Giving all that I've got
Everything that I can
Yet it feels not enough
To be superwoman

When he's awake
Wanting to play
Do I leave him alone
To get on with my day?
There are dishes to wash
And floors to keep clean
But my baby is playing
I feel caught in between

Do I read, sing and build
And leave housework undone?
What's best for him?
My attention or clean home?
I'm left feeling frazzled
Overwhelmed by the stress
For it's all necessary

And I'm trying my best

When he goes down to rest
I'm left with a choice
Keep working hard
Or relax and rejoice?
I could catch up on TV
Or maybe a nap
But there's washing to hang
And I'm caught in the trap

When he bites down hard
And I yell out loud
Causing crying and fear
I face a storm cloud
Of pain, shame and horror
For upsetting my little one
But I'm only human
What else could I have done?

I wake up all night
I dry all his tears
I play and I comfort
From outside it appears
I'm a wonderful mother
My happy baby squeals
Such delight, it's clear
There's no need to feel
Guilty

Body

I used to look in the mirror
Grudgingly
Imperfection
Judgement
Looking for beauty
Is that bit too squishy?
Too bony?
Are my thighs thin enough?
Or my breasts round and perky?
But I was okay
Happy enough
Still with room for improvement
Then the test came back positive

Suddenly I was looking in the mirror
Scared
Anticipation
Uncertainty
Saying goodbye
To the body I knew
For surely the body I would get
Would have greater imperfections?
Stretch marks? Loose skin?
Extra kilos? Sagging breasts?
But it was changing for a good cause

Growing with life

Then I looked in the mirror
Wonder
Amazement
Gratitude
That I could be so lucky
To be carrying a healthy child
Surreal to not remember
That body I used to have
And that little voice still worrying
What will be left when this ends?
Who will I see in the mirror then?

Now I look in the mirror
Empowered
Strong
Beautiful
My body brought another person
Into the world
And nourishes him still
Arms that hold him close
Breasts that feed and comfort
An abdomen that held a life
And a beautiful scar to mark his arrival
No more judgement
I no longer see imperfection
I see my body
With admiration and love

Tiny King

Tiny King upon your throne
Six months gone by - how much you've grown!
For weeks now every time I eat
You try to grab my veg or meat
So I've pulled a bib over your head
Now it's time for weaning, baby-led
But suddenly with food of your own
You think it's more fun when it's thrown
The floor is covered at every meal
And I'm left cleaning while I kneel
Yes, Tiny King, you're mighty and strong
But I'm done with cleaning all day long!
Cucumber, carrot, tomato and beans
You squish them all to smithereens!
You need a bath after every dinner
But it's just because you're a beginner
So as you grow, please, for me
Learn to eat food properly!

Safe Place

I am your safe place
Your comfort in the night
Shielding you from harm
Holding you tight
Some might try to hurt you
As you grow
With words and cruel actions
But you'll always know
I'll fight any battle
You need me to fight
Even if I'm scared
I'll make sure you're alright
But I know, as your safe place
Sometimes you might choose
To attack with your feelings
Let anger run loose
You'll show me your heartache
Rage and sorrow
Because you know
I'll still love you tomorrow
So sleep now, my baby
As I watch your sweet face
Knowing now and forever
I'll be your safe place

Lullaby

Rest, little baby
And when you wake
Another day
Of memories we'll make
Close your eyes
And dream sweet dreams
Of wandering through forests
Or dancing in streams
The night may be dark
But you're here safe and warm
My arms will hold you
Through any storm
When once more the sun
Wakes and shines down on you
You'll tell me your dreams
And we'll make them come true

Little Wonders

The pealing of a silver bell
Tinkling water in a well
The sunrise song of flitting birds
A writer's most inspired words
Most wondrous thing I've ever found
His little laugh, that joyful sound

Sweet nectar from a honey bee
The brightest sunset one could see
A clear blue sky on summer's day
Fresh roses in artful array
Such beauty holds me in my place
When I look upon his perfect face

The glory of the Northern Lights
Sunrise after the darkest nights
The new hope of an illness healed
An artist's masterpiece revealed
These wonders become less worthwhile
When the whole world lights up with his smile

Dear Baby

Dear Baby,
As I write this
you're asleep in my bed
I think of these poems
and the words I have said
One day you'll be grown
and I hope that you read this
These first months with you
are the ones I'll most miss
Even though it's been hard
and at times we've both cried
I see how far we've come
and it fills me with pride
From my tiny, new squish
to this bright-eyed young boy
As you've grown every day
you have filled me with joy
You're my dream come true
Everything I could ask for
When you smile or giggle
you leave me aching for more
Your laugh is the brightest
sound in my day
When I go out without you
I just wish I could stay

For each moment without you
hurts my heart
Since you grew in my belly
we're not meant to be apart
I know every Mum thinks
she's the luckiest one
But I've known that I am
since your life begun
While some of these poems
show a dark point of view
Every moment is worth it
because I have you
So if you're reading
just in case it's not clear
you should know with all my heart
I love you, my dear

Loss

It felt like tearing my heart out
I couldn't breathe, couldn't think
"I'm not seeing the growth we'd expect"
"I'm so sorry, there's no heartbeat"
Over and over, replayed in my head
Driving home through blurry eyes
But home offers no comfort
This storm can't be real
Wake up, wake up
Is it possible to pull out your own heart?
Would that make the pain stop?
"It wasn't meant to be"
"Sometimes these things just happen"
Shut up, shut up
I can't hear any more
Hands on my little bump
Instinctively trying to protect
They want to remove it
They want to tear my baby away
I can't bear it
I want to say no
I want to keep my baby
He should be safe with me
But he's already gone
And I'm falling apart

What If?

I woke up and you were gone
Surprised, I felt relief
I'd expected uncontrolled sadness
Instead there was calm and peace
In the days and weeks that followed
There was calm mixed with thunderstorms
Still peace alongside moments of hurt
Then the question began
What if?

What if I had ask more questions?
What if I had trusted my gut?
What if I had been stronger?
Would you still be here?

Would I be feeling you kicking?
Would I see you growing on scans?
Would I still be planning for your arrival?
Would I be showing by now?
What would the future hold?

Would you look just like your brother?
Would you love cars and ducks and balls?
What would it be like to kiss your head
And tuck you in at night?

What if I had done something
That could have kept you here?
There's no way to know, and I never will
But still I ask
What if?

Memory Box

Little box full of memories
All I have of you
The things I can't let go of
And I'm not sure I want to
That stick that showed a positive
With a perfect, pink line
The moment I first loved you
That's when you became mine
Photos of my baby bump
Your big brother so excited
Ready for a sibling
But that love goes unrequited
I made you a little beanie
That would have fit your tiny head
It sits there now, unworn
In the box beside my bed
Some artwork and precious words
To help me make it through
And right on top, your ashes
All that remains of you

www.ingramcontent.com/pod-product-compliance
Lightning Source LLC
Chambersburg PA
CBHW071456150726
48000CB00006B/2589